A Momentary Glory

WESLEYAN POETRY

▬ ▬ ▬

ALSO BY HARVEY SHAPIRO

The Eye, 1953

Mountain, Fire, Thornbush, 1961

Battle Report, 1966

This World, 1971

Lauds & Nightsounds, 1978

The Light Holds, 1984

National Cold Storage Company, 1988

A Day's Portion, 1994

Selected Poems, 1997

How Charlie Shavers Died and Other Poems, 2001

Poets of World War II (editor), 2003

The Sights Along the Harbor: New and Collected Poems, 2006

A Momentary Glory

HARVEY SHAPIRO

LAST POEMS

Glory

Edited by
Norman Finkelstein

WESLEYAN UNIVERSITY PRESS
MIDDLETOWN, CONNECTICUT

WESLEYAN UNIVERSITY PRESS

Middletown CT 06459

www.wesleyan.edu/wespress

© 2014 Estate of Harvey Shapiro

All rights reserved

Manufactured in the United States of America

Designed and typeset in Albertina and

Calluna Sans by Eric M. Brooks

Wesleyan University Press is a member of
the Green Press Initiative. The paper used in
this book meets their minimum requirement
for recycled paper.

*This project is supported in part by a grant from
the National Endowment for the Arts.*

Library of Congress Cataloging-in-Publication Data

Shapiro, Harvey, 1924–2013.

[Poems. Selections]

A momentary glory: last poems / Harvey Shapiro;
edited by Norman Finkelstein.

pages; cm. — (Wesleyan poetry series)

ISBN 978-0-8195-7489-3 (cloth: alk. paper) —

ISBN 978-0-8195-7495-4 (ebook)

I. Finkelstein, Norman, 1954– II. Title.

PS3537.H264A6   2014

811'.52 — dc23   2014003076

5 4 3 2 1

CONTENTS

▬ ▬ ▬

ACKNOWLEDGMENTS

Grateful acknowledgment is made to the editors of the following publications, in which some of the poems in this volume first appeared:

> *Bomb*: "Key West," "The Mother of Invention," "Dejection," "Oppen"
>
> *The Brooklyn Rail*: "Bush Poem," "City Poem," " Hospital Poem"
>
> *Hanging Loose*: "The Keys," "Brief Lives," "During the Second World War," "Pardoned"
>
> *TSR: The Southampton Review*, Vol. 11, No. 1, Summer 2008: "Departures"

I also wish to acknowledge the assistance of Kathryn Levy and Julia Sheehan in tracking down and determining the original publication sources of some of the poems that were found in Harvey's files. Many thanks to Michael Heller, old and dear friend of both Harvey and me, for reading and responding to the manuscript. To Galen Williams, whose love and devotion to Harvey was a constant throughout the time I knew him, thanks seem beside the point. As usual, Harvey said it best: "The gifts tumble from you all day."

EDITOR'S INTRODUCTION

In his author's note to *The Sights Along the Harbor: New and Collected Poems* (2006), Harvey Shapiro tells us that "the poems included here constitute the body of my work as I now see it. I count myself a lucky survivor and am pleased, as I hope readers will be, with what I've done with my time." Harvey carried on, still a lucky survivor, for another seven years. He passed away on January 7, 2013, just a few weeks before his eighty-ninth birthday, after being hospitalized for a number of months. Harvey had appointed me his literary executor in 2002, a couple of years after we had met. I was deeply moved, and a little overwhelmed, by the trust he put in me, coming in, as it were, rather late in the story. But he was pleased by what I had written about him, a long essay on the Jewish dimension of his work that first appeared in *Religion and Literature* and later was revised for my book on Jewish American poetry, *Not One of Them in Place*. (The title, not incidentally, comes from Harvey's poem "The Six Hundred Thousand Letters.") In the spring of 2002, he and his partner, Galen Williams, visited us in Cincinnati, and he gave a wonderful reading at Xavier. Otherwise, I would see Harvey on my trips to New York, and we would speak by phone regularly. Though he would tell me how his work was coming along, especially during that period when he was assembling *The Sights Along the Harbor*, he did not usually share his new poems with me. About twenty pages of new poetry appears in *Sights*; after its publication, I knew he was continuing to write at a leisurely pace, and he would casually mention poems forthcoming in one publication or another. My impression, therefore, when I went to his apartment in Brooklyn Heights a week after his death to look over his papers, was that I would find only a handful of poems beyond the ones that he had published since *Sights* had appeared.

As it turns out, I was utterly mistaken. Harvey had left behind a mass of manuscript pages in two file folders. I found drafts of the dozen or so poems that had appeared in periodicals, but they were mixed together with close to a hundred pages of new work. These pages, apparently printed from Harvey's laptop, were undated, but from internal evidence, I could tell that most of the poems had been written in the last six years. I realized quickly that there was a book here that needed to be shaped, and that Harvey was probably looking toward such a book before he entered the hospital for the last time. I spent two days on Montague Street. There on the thirty-third floor, with the apartment's magnificent views looking south across Brooklyn and west across lower Manhattan and the harbor, I sorted through the files, keeping most of the work and setting aside only those pages that seemed unfinished or still in the process of revision. Most of the pages were either completely clean or very lightly emended in Harvey's hand. A word might be cut or a line break altered, and in each case it struck me as just the right decision. I returned to Cincinnati, and a week later, Galen mailed me photocopies of the poems.

Organizing the manuscript proved relatively straightforward. In these poems, Harvey's overlapping subjects and themes remain the same as in the past, as readers familiar with his work will quickly see. There are poems about the places where he spent his last years, wry observations of city life, and of the Hamptons, and of the Florida Keys. There are poems based on his service in World War II (in 2003, the Library of America published the anthology that Harvey edited, *Poets of World War II*). There are love poems—Harvey is one of our great erotic poets. There are poems concerning some of the poets who meant the most to him, and of the writing life. And there are many poems of the sort that I consider an updated version of wisdom literature, suffused with Jewish irony and compassion, often anecdotal and bordering on the parabolic. But in all of the poems in this book, to an even greater extent than the work in *How Charlie Shavers Died* (2001) and the new poems section in *Sights Along the Harbor*, there is an intensity, an urgency, and a deep, meditative awareness that I find quietly astonishing.

These last poems constitute a sustained act of inspired writing, the passionate outpouring of a brilliantly gifted poet in the face of age, illness, and mortality. Their language is charged with unprecedented gravitas. Yet the work is as edgy as ever, and Harvey never abandons the supple, even jazzy wit that is central to his style. The verbal economy, the razor-sharp lineation, the perfectly timed presentation of detail that are his trademarks—all are subtly at work here, never flashy, still in the service of a poetic sensibility in search of what Harvey always called "the way." Rabbi Nachman's vision of the world as a narrow bridge, about which Harvey first wrote many years ago, appears one last time. Yet the fear of crossing that bridge is all but gone, and a great calm and acceptance of the world and its "momentary glory" prevails. And not only of the world, but of its Author. As Harvey declares in "Psalm,"

...before you
close your Book of Life, your Sefer Hachayim,
remember that I always praised your world
and your splendor and that my tongue
tried to say your name on Court Street in Brooklyn.
Take me safely through the Narrows to the sea.

Here then is Harvey Shapiro's Book of Life, his Sefer Hachayim.

Norman Finkelstein
Cincinnati, Ohio
May 2013

A Momentary Glory

THE OLD MAN HAS ONE THOUGHT
AND THEN ANOTHER

— — —

1
Let's go out
and fart in the sunlight.

Let's go to the playground
and check out the young mothers.

2
My eyes are blurred, and Louis
has burned his whole left arm
because, he says, he fainted in his house
and when he came to there was
a smell of something burning
and for some reason he picked up
a broom and began sweeping
and then a flame shot up his arm.
He's in good hands, he says, cheerfully.
I think we should close ranks
but there aren't any ranks to close.

3
The way women
in ancient Chinese poems
part the silk curtains
to see the lonely moon,

and feel better for it,
I see these streets.

4

Nicholas Magallenes and Maria Tallchief
are still doing "Firebird" in my head.
Music and dance and someday I know
I will find the words, the way Orpheus
stepped so carefully toward the light
carrying the song with him, losing the girl.

5

A young woman gets on the jitney.
The beauty of milky-white jugs
fills the bus. The green fields
are brighter.

6

In my eightieth year, I lost my luck.
I lost my luck and I lost my talent.
Now wherever I go, the sky is blank.
Whoever you are I take no interest.

7

Chou Chou, little cabbage.
I learned that endearment
in a bordello in Montreal
in the summer of '46.
The pimp, who doubled as the madam,
wore a pink kimono.

I was back from the wars,
still a student — of love, I guess,
and all the mysteries.

8
Sometimes at night I
try to remember who I
am. Then I forget
and there is no one to re-
mind me except my mute book.

9
On my desk is a small Buddha
and an Indian goddess of creativity
and in my head is Yahweh.
Son of man, Son of man, he says to me.
Get all the help you can.

10
My own lost life
is looking for me now,
at four in the morning,
blundering through the halls,
opening doors. It's my younger self,
confused, desperate, wanting
another chance. For what? I ask,
for what? knowing all the while
there is nothing I can do for him —
I'm too old, too infirm
and the girl is gone.

FOR WILLIAM CARLOS WILLIAMS

— — —

My rhetoric imagines you as your rhetoric says you.
You are in the city, drinking coffee,
a morning break. The poem in your head
is neighborly to all you see. Those who
sit next to you are not foreign to your lines.
Impure identities, they fill your poem with essences.
You do not build tombs for posterity
but open spaces where we can breathe
intelligence and the pain of love.
The bread of life is what we die to taste.
I taste it in your poems.

REZNIKOFF

— — —

When the words won't come right
Charles would do what?
He never told me. High-laced black
shoes. Went out to a poetry conference
in the west for five days and never
shat. So he complained to me on his
return. Late afternoon, and he decided,
since I was leaving, to walk down from
his place in the 70s to Times Square
where he could purchase, at his favorite
kiosk, his copy of the *Times Literary Supplement*.
Fortunately, I thought, he stumbled when
he first hit the street so I was able
to persuade him to take a bus downtown.
Waved to me from the window.
Goodbye, Charles.
Told me once that he had no use for
Zukofsky's work — too obscure.
He was after a Chinese clarity. He said
two things Oppen, Louis, Rakosi and he
had in common: they couldn't get published
and they admired the Do's and Don'ts
Ezra Pound was publishing in *Poetry*.

OPPEN

— — —

"An instrument of torture"
said the poet George Oppen
when a Catholic chaplain
waved the cross above his face
where he lay wounded
on a battlefield in France.
It was the answer of a man
who called things by their right names.

It may have been
a killing offense.
I'm so sorry.
Which is why
in my dream tonight
I left the dinner table
to write a note of apology
for Louis Zukofsky
who couldn't be there.
He understood
the limits of language
and the limits of sanctity
and would have known
why my anger
rose like Achilles
because my chance
to say something
to those who were there,
not many
as it turned out,
had been so
carelessly thrown away.

When I asked Wallace Stevens how he got his work done—
this was at Bard, in 1949, he was there for his first honorary degree—
he said: "On weekends I stay in my wing of the house
and my wife stays in hers. We meet only for Sunday dinner."
I savored the style of it at once: a certain kind of house
and a certain kind of marriage, and the steely intelligence
of that blue-eyed, Prussian-haired, banker-like poet.

THE PEOPLE'S POET

He was so pleased
with the poverty of his imagination.
It made him
brother to everyone.

ON A REJECTION NOTE FROM PAUL MULDOON

— — —

Paul writes that he wants me
"at my most exhilarating."
Paul, let's be reasonable.
I'm eighty-six. I've probably
been at my most exhilarating.
I can remember when I was
exhilarated maybe three or four
times a week. Isabel did that.
And I was exhilarating in turn,
so she said. And I could
transfer that energy to the page.
Now I can be cunning, skillful,
maybe even wise. Let's settle
for that. Yours truly, Harvey

HOMAGE

▬ ▬ ▬

> *The ice-white*
> *eternal promise*
> *of a new moon.*
>
> JAMES SCHUYLER

When you feel absolutely nothing.
Bone-dead, brain-dead.
A body that eats and shits.
Then to read lines set down
in honest emotion — pleasure
or pain — lines in which
the emotion finds its way into words
that spark a perception
of something truly seen, can lift the heart.

LINES (1)

━ ━ ━

I am surrounded by easy-to-read
enjoyable poetry. Every poem
tells a story about an American place,
like a barn or a skating rink
or the inside of an American poet's
head, with its own barn
or its own skating rink. And I'm sitting
in the middle of this profusion
of images, a splay of old *Saturday
Evening Post* covers, hungering
for war, pornography and death.

NOW I WRITE

—— —— ——

Now I write
to prove to myself
that there is nothing
for me to write about
and that the time I spend
reading, watching television
or just staring into space
is only the rich, well-deserved
leisure of old age.

How to write poems of perfect resignation
when what's on tap is rage, enmity
and a wish to do it all over again
but this time get it right.

Because I am someone
on whom you can't rely,
the witnesses are many.
I was chosen to write these poems
that pretend to experience love
and awe of creation — but only
to solicit a sigh, some sympathy,
a free pass to what is there.

ON MY BOOK

I have preserved my words
as if they contained wisdom
or luck or happiness.
But I know well what they contain
and I never take up my book.

WRITING

＝ ＝ ＝

Writing, to put distance
between myself
and what I have written.

So I am free to start another life.

With that, he rose from his desk
and left the room.

to which he returns tomorrow.

I wrote two poems in my sleep.
They seemed quite good to me.
Whoever took them down
I'm sure will return them to me.

THE POEM

Is an Egyptian
ship of the dead,
everything required
for life stored
in its hold.

DURING THE SECOND WORLD WAR

I stood at the door of a B-17
with one engine on fire.
I had been told to get ready
to bail out. Beneath me were
the snow-covered mountains
of Yugoslavia. Around me
was nothing but air.
I wanted to stand there forever.

MEMORIAL DAY

The guy in basic training
who did orgasms with his neck.

The guy who sat next to me
at a briefing and wept
when the target was announced:
Berlin. He was almost home, this
was his 35th mission, and was
afraid to die so far from home.

I am trying to recollect faces
in the flickering shadow of my war
so I can tell Telemachus,
who couldn't care less.

AN AMERICAN LIFE

— — —

The tunes I hear in my eighties
I first heard in my teens.
Like, "You must remember this,
a kiss is just a kiss,
a sigh is just a sigh.
The fundamental things apply
as time goes by."
When I was twenty,
the words had changed to
"You must remember this,
the flak can't always miss,
there's someone's going to die.
The fundamental things apply
as flak goes by."
I sang them in Italy,
in the bars, between missions.
And here I am at eighty-five,
the tune on the radio, driving along,
caught in a time warp that sings.

DISCOURSE ON EDUCATION

I was trained in war.
At nineteen, I could put together
a 50-caliber machine gun
blindfolded. Now I work
in verse, and hope to do
something commensurate.

FOGGIA, ITALY

He walks to the edge of the airfield
to get aviation fuel for the steel drum
rigged up in his tent as a stove.
Rutted mud underfoot but the spring sun
on his face feels good. Low mountains in the distance
through clear air. Everything shines because
yesterday he was on a mission and today,
and probably for the next few days,
he can ignore the early morning whistle followed
by the cry of H Hour. Turn over, go back to sleep.
Get up and walk in the beautiful world.

THE OLD WAR

▬ ▬ ▬

Now that I think of it
I saw no damage.
I saw planes going down,
flames,
steel piercing steel
but no dead bodies
piled up or strewn
across fields.

The bombed railroad yards
in the Austrian snow.
The thud of the exploding shells
under the plane. The jagged
hole suddenly opening beside
my head. Is that what I know?

It was on a bombing mission near Vienna
when his oxygen mask clogged
and he slipped into a deep, warm sleep
that the radar operator, sitting across from him,
had to pull him out of, feeding him
pure oxygen from a tank.

So these were death's portals,
he understood, when in his eighties
in the hospital room he again
began to give up the ghost.
It's all in Whitman's threnody:
"Come lovely and soothing death."

SONG

The day I almost died
was near Vienna when I was
nineteen. And the day
I almost died was over
Regensburg when I was twenty.
And the day I almost died
was in a Southampton hospital
when I was eighty. Maestro, is
this a song that never ends?

THE TRANSACTION

I have no more use for it
than it has for me
but we go on dumbly together,
breathing in and breathing out.

ALEXANDRA

▬ ▬ ▬

She called, stoned, from Cooperstown.
There was nothing on the TV.
Outside, whatever was inhabiting the land
had gone to sleep somewhere over Colorado.
A harmonica would be corny but
it's the way the music tends.

LYDIA

— — —

This praise is for you
with your precise speech,
your naked eyes, the blue lights
coming on suddenly.

CYNTHIA

— — —

Reach in, she said,
and get some juice.
That was happiness.

KING KONG'S WONG

You never actually see it in the movie.
When he's astride the Empire State,
batting at planes, it makes sense that
he's too busy to shake it at the city
like a club. And when
he's got Fay Wray in the palm
of his hand, you know it's reaching
gigantic proportions,
but below the screen.

NIGHTPIECE
— — —

She said, You hurt me.
Would you get off
my fucking bed.
I had my arms
around her
and I kept them there.
I knew I could do that
because
nothing mattered to her
anymore.

Drear, bleared and boiled,
she comes to bed.
Who am I to judge?
The pain washes over us,
the surf of years.

A STORY

— — —

She places her hand in his hand
as if both were erotic objects.
It feels that way to him
when she places her hand there.

When he put his trust
in the long line of her back
bent from him in sleep.

She said to him:
I'll let you know
when to feel insecure.
And she did.

BRIEF LIVES

Is it true that I am left
sitting in front of the courthouse
while she has ascended to the empyrean?
I close *The New York Review of Books*
remembering how sad I was
fucking her up the ass (her choice)
the eve of our breakup,
and how the next morning at the
Peekskill station she stroked my
shoulders in sympathy for my loss.
Now I am descending ever deeper
into old age, as into her darkness.

BROOKLYN

This evening, for example,
when the sky cleared, the light
at the end of Atlantic Avenue
over the water —
so that everyone crossing the street
turned for a moment,
touched by something.

TO THE BROOKLYN ACADEMY OF MUSIC

We were speaking about the children.
What do you want for the children.
The younger boy has a clogged tongue;
he can barely say "cement."
I address you as a parent
interested in improvement.
Meaningful songs in the Academy
of Music, heavenly hints,
bread for poets who walk past
bridges. There are men
fishing in the Channel almost
the entire year. I have a sense
of place in Brooklyn,
of precise geographical position.
People invited to dinner
frequently cross water.
On Kane Street (how I enjoy
the name), in the old synagogue,
I purge my sins with the remnant.
All this is provided. And
now I have to put in the music
for the boy with the clogged tongue.

LINES (2)
— — —

In the 42nd Street station
of the 7th Avenue IRT
a black man with a silver sax
plays "Amazing Grace"
as I come down the steps — 11 PM —
having just seen *Hamlet* with Bill
and Jennifer, carrying in my head
the empty stage, empty
but pulsating with the energies of the play,
light waves radiating from the bare floorboards.
An unquiet death the sweet prince suffered
and despite Fortinbras and his ranked men
the chaos is so vast
words won't staunch it, as if the writer at the end
knew this was all he could do.
Such knowledge is what this grimy subway platform
bespeaks every day. I believe it.

7TH AVENUE IRT

The way summer settles in.
Dogs lapping water.
My feet breathing through their soles.
The 7th Avenue IRT.
A testing place for the old.
Over each crumpled form
Stands a cop like a blue headstone.

TIMES SQUARE

Nothing fraught. High intensity
like high anxiety, just another name
for comedy. So let the battering begin,
the discordant voices, each issuing
from its own bedlam. And the sulfurous sky
smiling benignly on every living thing.

IN THE CITY

The shit will hit the fan
momentarily.

The massive skyline of Manhattan —
a vaudeville backdrop before which
I pivot and turn.

THE KEYS

Light everywhere.
Wave glint, palm glint.
On rock and on sand.
Light nesting
in the Florida Keys
as if the holy shaper
like an old Jew
gathered it here to watch
while he sipped his soup.

KEY WEST

At the corner of Simonton and Amelia
there is a small junkyard that is
as beautiful to me as the deep
blue sea stretching from here to Cuba.
It has an arching tree over it
and its shards of old cars, tractors,
boating gear shine in the tropic sun
but with an American splendor
like rolling waves of grain. How odd
to have been taught to respond to
junk by my culture, and with
a patriotic fervor, so that the colors
red, white, and blue blaze through the rust.

FLORIDA

▬ ▬ ▬

The sea beating
against the parking lots.

REAL ESTATE

Approaching East Hampton,
you think you see a barn and a tractor
but it turns out to be
a new house and a bulldozer.

DEER

— — —

The deer sifting
through the small cropped grass
looking for a line by Thomas Wyatt
to house him in shivers
sensing he is only a few steps
from roadkill.

SUBURBAN NOTE

The deer don't startle anymore.
They turn from me in boredom,
edging on loathing: that a grown man
who has seen war and the destruction of cities
should bestir himself to keep them from their food.

ROCKPORT

The band concert at evening in the gazebo.
Sailboats clustered along the shore.
The listeners, mostly locals and their children.
Sousa's name said with reverence.

PARIS

It is winter in Paris and it is raining.
Gray sky, gray stones, gray birds
scooting over the Seine. On the Isle
the shops would be bright, except it's Sunday,
so they are not. A Parisian melancholy
settles over me. Why then do I think of Bob and Donna
in their kitchen in Brooklyn, staring
into their small, wet backyard,
waiting for the redemption of the Gowanus Canal
so they can paddle into the sunrise?

IN PRAGUE

— — —

In Prague I go to visit
Franz Kafka's grave.
A small plot, very small, I think,
to hold father, mother and son.
And only one headstone
on which Papa Herman gets top billing!
The caretaker tells me: "You know
the old Jews from Prague,
the few who are left,
when they come here they say to me
'Franz should have listened to his father.'
I don't think they're right.
After all, he's famous.
Isn't that so? But
I don't dare contradict them."

QUESTIONS

— — —

What is it you thought you knew?

When?

When you were sure of something, when you believed
the words would lift you up.

Lift me up?

Yes, as in a trance, as in a fever of believing.

Ah, that was the booze.

No, that was before the booze.

Well, I was very young. I was intoxicated.

And now?

And now I work at it. A little light before the darkness.

GREEN

When I entered the slough of despond,
wearing my green underwear,
I suddenly became aware
that nobody else was there.
So I sat alone in my chair
and admired my green underwear.

MOZART POEM

Of course, this will lead to that,
lyrically to that,
and so beautifully to that. Turns
and returns, and turns in a different direction
so that some basic law, like gravity,
is constantly defied.

WORLD

To make the world perfect and full of splendor.
Was this indeed anybody's wish?
I look around me and inside me.

In my own night ward
Drinking slowly, smoking slowly,
The city at my back.
Both of us making
The long recovery to morning.

IN THE BEGINNING

The green leaves against the blue sky
look so primal, as if these were the first colors
after the dark shadow slid from the vast abyss.

DAN, AGE 10, EXPLAINS

━ ━ ━

1

You can't just die in Brooklyn.
You have to be killed or mugged.
You die in Miami.

2

I can't find it
Owing to the
Darkness of the world.

BUSH POEM

The significant end was approaching.
Nobody said as much on television
but everybody felt it. Maybe
that was because the President was a
religious man and was transmitting
unconsciously to the people something
he deeply believed. It was not the mounting
deaths or the sinking dollar. It was not
anything political or national. Scripture,
in those dark days, glowed like uranium.

It's President Bush's birthday, and in the packed hall
Terri Schiavo is singing to George Bush
with the same voice Marilyn Monroe used to sing
Happy Birthday to Jack Kennedy. When suddenly
a terrified voice calls out: "She can't be singing,
she's dead." And President Bush steps forward
and says: "She's singing because she loves me."

HOT SUMMER

The bird feeders are empty
but it is much too hot to feed the birds.
And the squirrels often steal the seed,
which raises my blood pressure.
So forget the birds. And forget immortality
and the durability of art. I'd rather
be cool right now than immortal tomorrow.
All of the above is very clear to me.
Everything else is a mess.

＿ ＿ ＿

A bird in a tree said Debit debit.
Another day lost in anger.

BIRDS

The way the birds shy from the feeder
for hours after you've filled it
as if hours of wind and sun were
needed to clear the blood scent
from Cain's offering.

Like a boy again,
daydreams are my accomplishment.

REMEMBERING
━ ━ ━

All those tears.
Every night she tells the story.
All those tears.
Is the soil in which the dead lie
so dry it needs this?
A small chorus around the dinner table
and the speaker, with a single light
on her face. All those tears.

FRIDAY

What happened to the lady with the gifts?
She doan come here no mo
said Henry or Harvey.
There ain't nothing doin
on field or stream or in the broad blue ocean,
which looks increasingly like home
to the ancient mariner, even in winter,
with a lone gull scudding the wind-swept waves.

BOOK GROUP

━ ━ ━

We read a book ostensibly
about the Holocaust in which
six million were killed, babies
had their skulls bashed against
the wall, an entire culture
was wiped out, leaving only
the vaudeville Jews of America
and the critic in the group says
the theme is survival and
everyone cries paradox! paradox!

I am in a warm room
but I can sense the cold
gripping bushes and trees
and ground in its white sheath.
Where can I find perfect silence
except in this world.

THE DISTANCE
▬ ▬ ▬

Prayer, as in:
my silence approaches
God's silence.
The distance to be covered
is so immense
that there is time
to live my life
peacefully.

RABBI NACHMAN'S PARABLE

␣␣␣

It was the king's son, naked under the table,
convinced he was a turkey, gobbling bones and bread.
The king coaxed, the queen coaxed. Maidens
were brought from as far away as Persia.
Still he roosted and dreamed fowl dreams.
A wise man stepped forward to do the work.
He stripped, and under the table introduced himself,
just another turkey. They gobbled together.
At a signal, a shirt was thrown to the wise man.
Did you think, he said, that a turkey
cannot wear a shirt and still be a turkey?
There followed pants, the rest of clothing, food.
Then the wise turkey said, Do you think a turkey
must sit under the table? You can be a turkey
and sit right at the table. So they did.

FOR ADIN

— — —

Classifying the whales, Melville's angelology,
in the mouth of my almost-four grandson,
teaching me out of the deep.

DEJECTION

The man is dead.
Sock him in the head.
Put him in his bed.
Fill him full of lead.
Show us where he bled.
See his soul has fled.
His books aren't read.
The man is dead.

THE MOTHER OF INVENTION

— — —

On my desk are the bills from the living
and in my sleep are the bills from the dead.

"Emptiness is the mother of invention"
says my fortune cookie. July 23, 2010.

Brooklyn. I walk in the slow rain,
never less accomplished, never happier.

Why should I doubt the world has meaning
when even in myself I see mysterious purposes.

A crow drops down for a moment,
black, rabbinical garb, croaking Kaddish.

PLANNING

In my final years
I have moved into a basement apartment
so I can get used to the steps
of the living above me
and to their sweet weight.

HONESTLY
— — —

You'd think he would have noticed
when the story ended. It was when
the blue rushed in and then the dark
and there was no one to turn to.

Where was the wisdom that was supposed
to accompany old age? Probably at the
bottom of the Cracker Jack box,
way at the bottom, his fingers groping
for it in a great rush of time.

DRUMS

Kettle drums like Beethoven announcing fate
or the way you came into my life
or the way you left it.

IN ARGUMENT

When the face that was so beautiful
turns ugly in argument
and the accusations fly—
you always—
then I know that death will come
leaving me as ignorant as ever.

THE OLD JEW

Who would have thought
his taste for pickled herring
would outlast
his taste for women.

LINES (3)

1

Corazón, o corazón. Let the heart
weep for this world, and let nothing
stay it in its weeping.
It is all I wanted to do with my life —
to sing with a harsh throb in my throat
like a flamenco singer. Now
I have the age for it.

2

The doctors confer
and try a new drug.
The surgeon waits in the wings.
I say to myself, Time's on my side
and then the fat lady sings.

3

When the sun sinks
my spirit sinks.
Is age turning me
into a sensitive plant —
a man who has seen war
and the destruction of cities?

4

I walked these streets
pushing sons in a stroller.
Now I stumble down them alone.

5

This poem was born in pain
and exists in pain
and will expire in pain.
Pain and silence.

6

In that old study
where I used to sit
the family is sleeping beneath me.
Not where I am now
in the wilderness of time
where the words sting
like wind-driven rain.

7

In that great loneliness
that is the world,
in that great loneliness
from which we are gathered
as light is gathered and dispersed,
as starlight is gathered and dispersed among us,
so that we can see each other, though the dark
is immense and will cover us
as light covered the deep.

DEPARTURES

— — —

1

A great ship steaming
out of the mouth of the Hudson,
shrouded in fog,
past Battery, past Governor's Island,
now blocking my view of the Lady.
A stately, silent exit
(because so distant?)
while the traffic of the BQE
buzzes beneath me.
If I could send my eighty-three years
out to sea like that,
with all that I've done wrong,
I could lay my head
beside the golden door.

2

And now we enter
the forest of Arden
where everything is possible
and the most haunting lyrics
are sung by fools and clowns,
and where I want to be.

3
Nobility of utterance
was never my strong suit,
nor nobility of style.
I came to the table
in my bathrobe
and said what the night
had taught me.

4
I've become bone-clean
and scentless.
There is nothing
for birds and small dogs
to pick over. I've become
a scarab for the muse
to wear around her neck.

2007

Amid the fires of the last century—
the cities and the Jews—
stands the Angel of Death
mighty as in the Plague Years
and in ascendency still.

THE OFFICE

— — —

Death with his deletion mark
went through the office. Bob Lewis,
Barney Lefferts, Sherwin Smith were
the first to fall. The copy moved
as before, through different desks,
through different sets of hands
and nobody looked up.

IN THE OFFICE

My friend said,
These are the years in which
you should be kind to yourself.
We were standing in the office
between a row of desks.
Sunlight scattered on the windowpane.
We have been young and now we are old
in this office. He was offering me his wisdom
because my case was difficult.

HOSPITAL POEM

— — —

I have little blood left
and a little money.
When they're gone
I'm out of here.
I have sat among the wheel-chaired dead
of America, their diapers clean, their smiles bright.
All of them, as in life, huddled before the giant screen.
Helicopter traffic
at the hospital.
The night has wings
but also wounds and death.

SELF-PITY

Now my life is spent sleeping and shitting
only I don't shit into a toilet
but into a plastic bag.
And I don't shit from my anus
but from part of my colon that extrudes
from a swollen area above and
to the right of my umbilicus.
It looks like a misplaced breast.
The extruding colon has the shape and color
of a young man's cock. Removing the bag
when it is full and replacing it with a fresh one
is something I do maybe three times a day.
I also try to write, usually simple descriptions
like this one. I don't seem to use rhyme
or meter much, perhaps because my matter
is unpleasantly formless like my shit.
The closest I've come to a lyric in months
is an adaptation of some lines by Yeats:
I carry the moon in a silver cup.
My shit in a plastic bag.

LINES (4)

He was too tired to look up "escutcheon."
So this was the end of the story.

LUXURY OF TIME

— — —

Like the Holy One
Creating worlds
And desolating them
All morning.

The piece of myself I must deliver
to death I have not found.
It is in the poems, surely.
It stands there, ready for my death,
naming me.

PARDONED

I don't have to spend
my eternity in Queens
because the family plot in Queens
is as crowded as a subway
at rush hour. Instead,
I can choose my own ground
and my own tree
and my own crow to croak Kaddish.

CITY POEM

1

Bare but numinous trees,
even in winter, even in the city,
feeding on cement but bearing
the whole burden of the air
and the misery that seeps from the stones
and from those who wander among them.

2

Of all the different kinds of light
I like it best when dark comes on,
near-dark, on the river and the town
when the lights along the bridge
become jewel-like and shine for me
as they did before, when my heart was whole
and I began my journeying.

3

Memories, like ancient ruins, I visit them.
Lost in the city a lifetime.
Street dark with rain and black umbrellas.
In Brooklyn , sky lightens over water.
Savage gulls ride the current, eyes bright for spoil.
Fever, like the edge of a desert.
To see the dawn and the broad ocean.

POETICS

In the argument over rhetoric
I am always for the lofty
but somehow wind up opting for the low.
Is that because Rezi speaks in me still,
his Jewish moral concerns
which he wanted set down lucidly,
matter-of-factly,
with the lucidity, never prettiness
of Du Fu and Li Po.

FOR GALEN

The way the gifts tumble from you all day
because you are a woman.
I never get a chance to say thank you
before you're on to the next:
a turn, a smile, a hand on my sleeve.

BRIGHT WINTER

▬ ▬ ▬

from the Hebrew of Avraham ben Yitzhak (1883–1950)

Pure, hard, white world.
Yesterday the north wind
scattered the lingering fog
that had once seemed blind, unending.
Today the wind slacks off.
Snow-glint on all sides.
A blue shadow of mountains and a pale sky
hover in that light
from multitudinous scales —
dark mineral, bright
with shining snow.
Far off, it twists
into the green distance.
It was there day ignited,
then spread in a halo of flames
as if the fractured ice
became a fractured sun.
My eyes shut,
my blood sings to me:
the world is pure.
Joined to the body of the world,
my heart's blood
streams beneath ice
in a country that is pure,
absolute, pure.

A MOMENTARY GLORY

This world is a momentary glory.
I never thought it would last forever
so I tried to get it down
in one notebook or another,
in one poem or another.
Somewhere you can find it.

PSALM

▬ ▬ ▬

I am still on a rooftop in Brooklyn
on your holy day. The harbor is before me,
Governor's Island, the Verrazano Bridge
and the Narrows. I keep in my head
what Rabbi Nachman said about the world
being a narrow bridge and that the important thing
is not to be afraid. So on this day
I bless my mother and father, that they be
not fearful where they wander. And I
ask you to bless them and before you
close your Book of Life, your Sefer Hachayim,
remember that I always praised your world
and your splendor and that my tongue
tried to say your name on Court Street in Brooklyn.
Take me safely through the Narrows to the sea.

HARVEY SHAPIRO was born in Chicago on January 27, 1924. His parents were religiously observant, Yiddish-speaking Russian Jewish immigrants who met and married in the United States. Like many Jewish American poets of his generation, Shapiro's first language was Yiddish. Shapiro's father was a businessman; his mother was a homemaker. The family moved to Manhattan when Shapiro was a boy, and then, during the Depression, to Woodmere, Long Island. He had one younger brother, who emigrated to Israel as a young man.

Shapiro began college at Yale but soon after enlisted in the Army Air Force to fight in World War II. His experiences in the war proved foundational to his poetic identity: he began reading poetry seriously while serving in the military, and he would return to the subject of the war throughout his writing life, eventually editing the anthology *Poets of World War II* (2003). He flew thirty-five missions as a B-17 tail gunner and was awarded the Distinguished Flying Cross. Returning to Yale after the war, he completed his bachelor's degree in English in 1947 and received a master's in American literature from Columbia in 1948. Although he began an academic career, teaching at Cornell and Bard, he soon chose to become a journalist, working at the *Village Voice, Commentary,* and the *New Yorker,* before taking a position at the *New York Times* in 1957. He worked at the *Times* until his retirement in 1995, holding various editorial positions at the *Times Magazine* and, from 1975 to 1983, serving as the editor of the *Book*

Review. In 1963, while working at the *Magazine,* he contacted the Southern Christian Leadership Conference and suggested that the next time Dr. Martin Luther King was arrested for leading civil rights protests, he should write a letter that the *Times* would publish. The result was one of King's most important pieces of writing, the "Letter from a Birmingham Jail." Ironically, Shapiro could not convince his superiors to publish the letter, and it appeared in other periodicals.

With journalism as his day job, Shapiro worked continually on his poetry, sometimes writing long into the night. His early work bore the mark of the formalism endorsed by the mid-century New Criticism, but he gradually turned to free verse, writing the short, jazz-inflected poems of momentary observation and sudden insight for which he became known. Beginning in 1953 with *The Eye,* he published his work at regular intervals, culminating in *The Sights Along the Harbor: New and Collected Poems* in 2006. Jewish culture, belief, and identity remain a constant in his poetry. Though he was not observant, the notion of a quest for belief, of searching for "the Way" (*halakhah*) is fundamental to his poetry. His book *Mountain, Fire, Thornbush* (1961) deals exclusively with Jewish themes, but he also turned to Jewish texts—the Bible, Midrash, Kabbalah, modern Jewish philosophy—in his later work as well. During the 1980s and '90s, he participated in the Genesis Seminar, a distinguished group of writers and scholars who met to read the Hebrew scriptures. From that seminar came the book *Congregation: Contemporary Writers Read the Jewish Bible* (1987), to which Shapiro contributed an essay on the Book of Joel.

Perhaps above all, Shapiro was a consummate poet of New York City (he lived in Brooklyn Heights for over fifty years), writing a wry, darkly ironic sort of urban wisdom literature. He felt a strong literary kinship with Walt Whitman, Hart Crane, and Frank O'Hara, but his closest connections, both poetically and personally, were to the Objectivist poets. William Carlos Williams was an important early influence; Shapiro and Williams corresponded and met at Yaddo in 1949, when both had summer residencies there. In New York, Shapiro became friends with Charles Reznikoff, Louis Zukofsky, and George Oppen. Both Zukofsky and Oppen lived for a time near Shapiro in Brooklyn; Oppen in particular served as a crucial mentor and role model. Shapiro was also close to other poets of what could be called the Objectivist milieu, including David Ignatow, Hugh Seidman, Michael Heller, and Armand Schwerner, often spending summers in the Hamptons near Heller and Schwerner. In later years, he would summer in Key West, where he was also part of a lively literary community.

Shapiro was married once and divorced; the couple had two sons, Saul and Daniel. Galen Williams was his companion during the latter part of his life; they lived in Brooklyn Heights and East Hampton. Although ailing from heart disease and related illnesses in his last years, Shapiro continued to write with extraordinary vigor and imagination, as the present volume amply proves. After being hospitalized for some months, he died in Manhattan on January 7, 2013.

A reader's companion to this volume is available at harveyshapiro.site.wesleyan.edu.

NORMAN FINKELSTEIN is a poet and literary critic.
His books of poetry include *Scribe* (2009), *Inside the Ghost
Factory* (2010), and the serial poem *Track,* which originally
appeared in three volumes and has been republished
in a one-volume edition (2012). His most recent critical
book is *On Mount Vision: Forms of the Sacred in Contemporary
American Poetry* (2010). He has written extensively about
Jewish American literature and modern American poetry,
especially poetry in the Objectivist tradition. Finkelstein
was born in New York City in 1954. He received a bachelor's
degree from Binghamton University and a doctorate from
Emory University. He is a professor of English at Xavier
University in Cincinnati, where he has taught since 1980.
He is also currently a research candidate at the Cincinnati
Psychoanalytic Institute.